Special Days

Mother's Day

Jillian Powell

HODDER
Wayland

An imprint of Hodder Children's Books

► Special Days ◄

Bonfire Night
Christmas
Easter
May Day
Mother's Day
Poppy Day

Editor: Carron Brown
Series design: Kate Buxton
Book designer: Joyce Chester
Illustrator: David Antram
Consultant: Norah Granger
First published in 1998 by Wayland Publishers Limited

This paperback edition published in 2002 by Hodder Wayland,
an imprint of Hodder Children's Books

British Library Cataloguing in Publication Data
Powell, Jillian
Mother's Day. – (Special Days)
1. Mother's Day – Juvenile literature
2. Mother's Day – United States – Juvenile literature
2. Mother's Day – Great Britain – Juvenile literature
I. Title II. Antram, David
394.2'62

ISBN 0 7502 4391 0

Typeset in England by Joyce Chester
Printed in Hong Kong

Picture Acknowledgments
The publishers would like to thank the following for allowing us to reproduce their pictures:
Bridgeman Art Library, London/Hereford City Museum and Art Gallery 23, /Musée Condé, Chantilly, France 9,
/Museo di San Marco dell'Angelico, Florence 18, /Penlee House Art Gallery and Museum, Penzance 15, /Novosti 10,
/Warrington Museum and Art Gallery, Lancs. 11; Eye Ubiquitous/Paul Seheult 24, 26; Getty Images 14, 22,
/Myrleen Cate 25, /Laurence Monneret 27, /Ian Shaw 5, /Jerome Tisne 4, 30; Image Bank *title page*.

Contents

Mother's Day   4

Beginnings   6

Mother Church   8

Mothering Sunday   10

A family day   12

Going 'a-mothering'   14

Gifts for mother   16

Simnel cake   18

White carnations   20

War-time   22

Cards   24

Flowers   26

Celebrating Mother's Day 28

Glossary   30

Timeline   31

Further information   31

Index   32

Mother's Day

Every year there is one special day
when we say thank you to our mothers
for all they do for us. In some countries,
Mother's Day is in March, but in some
countries it is in May.

▼ All over the world mothers wake up
to their special day.

Wherever we live, we send special cards to our mothers and give them gifts like flowers or chocolates. It is a way of showing our mothers how much we love them.

▲ Helping out is one way of showing mothers we care.

Beginnings

No one knows when the first special day for mothers took place. Long ago, people took gifts of food and flowers to holy places to say thank you to Mother Nature for all her goodness.

▼ These Roman women are carrying flowers to the temple of Juno.

People used to pray to Mother goddesses and take gifts to their temples. The Romans had a special day in March when women took flowers to a temple for the goddess Juno.

Mother Church

Hundreds of years ago, Christian people in Britain chose a day in March to visit their Mother Church. This was the most important church or cathedral in their part of the country.

▼ People often picked flowers while they walked to their Mother Church.

► This calendar from long ago shows people travelling to church on foot and horseback.

They walked many kilometres to take gifts and flowers to the church. The day they chose was the fourth Sunday during Lent, the forty days before Easter.

9

Mothering Sunday

Lent is when Christians remember the time Jesus Christ went without food for forty days. So for Christians Lent was a hard time when they were not allowed to enjoy meals or play sports or games.

▼ Jesus in the desert thinking about all the things he had to do.

▲ Lent was a time for reading the Bible and other quiet activities.

The day Christians visited their Mother Church was half-way through Lent, so they made it a special day and called it Mothering Sunday.

A family day

On Mothering Sunday, the whole family met together. They walked to church in the morning, then they had a special family meal at home.

They usually ate roast lamb or veal, then a plum or fig pudding with custard. They drank wine or beer they had made at home. Sometimes, the children drank frumenty, which was a milky drink with spices in it.

▼ A family meal on Mothering Sunday in Victorian times.

Going 'a-mothering'

In those days, many boys and girls had to leave home when they were still young to find work.

◀ Girls often worked as maids in big houses.

◀ Boys went to work in shops or learnt to make things.

Boys and girls had to work very hard and they did not have many holidays. On Mothering Sunday, they were given a day off to go 'a-mothering', which meant visiting their mothers.

Gifts for mother

Sons and daughters all went home to their families. They took their mothers little gifts like tea, linen or gloves. They picked spring flowers like violets and primroses on the way.

▼ A mother welcomes her children home. They have come to visit her with flowers and gifts.

Sometimes, the girls took a special cake which they had baked. Sometimes, the mistress of the house where they worked baked a cake for them. It was called a Simnel cake.

Simnel cake

Simnels are rich fruit cakes with marzipan on top. They can be round and flat, or baked in a star-shape. Sometimes, they are decorated with sugar flowers or eggs and the words 'Mother' or 'Mothering Sunday'.

▼ Jesus and his twelve disciples.

Eleven eggs on the cake are said to stand for all the disciples, except Judas who betrayed Jesus.

▲ Simnel cakes were kept to be eaten on Easter Day with a special Easter tea.

19

White carnations

In some countries, Mother's Day is in May. This began in 1907 when an American called Miss Anna Jarvis wanted to have a special day to remember her mother who had died.

▼ On Mother's Day people wore white carnations to church or, if their mothers were still alive, they wore red carnations.

She had a service in church and asked everyone who came to wear a white carnation. Soon after this, Americans named the second Sunday in May 'Mother's Day'.

War-time

During the Second World War, many American soldiers came over to Britain. They brought with them the idea of giving gifts and cards for mother's special day. People in Britain who had forgotten Mother's Day began to celebrate it again.

▼ American and British soldiers feeding pigeons in London during the Second World War.

For
MUMMY

With lots of Love
to the best Mummy
in the world.

LYCHGATE LTD. WORTHING.   HAND COLOURED   MADE IN GT. BRITAIN
P.C. 21.

They began sending Mother's Day cards. Some were shaped like aprons, spinning wheels or teapots to show how hard mothers worked in the home.

▲ A Mother's Day card from around fifty years ago.

23

Cards

Today, there are all sorts of cards
for Mother's Day. It is nice to make
your own Mother's Day card.

◄ Crayon
drawings make
colourful cards.

You can draw or paint a picture or design one on a computer screen. You can also make up the words that go inside to make it your special card.

▲ Writing or drawing on your own card makes it special.

Flowers

Flowers have always been important for Mother's Day. For florists, Mother's Day is one of the busiest days of the year.

They make up many bunches and baskets of flowers to send to mothers all over the world.

◀ Flowers make a special surprise gift.

In some places in Britain, children take flowers to be blessed in church before they give them to their mothers.

▲ A Mother's Day posy.

Celebrating Mother's Day

Mother's Day is a special day when we say thank you to our mothers and show them we are thinking of them.

We can give them treats like taking them breakfast in bed or helping with jobs. We can help to make them feel special on their special day.

▼ These children are going to surprise their mother with their home-made cards and gifts.

Glossary

Blessed   Made holy by a service in church.

Carnations   Garden flowers that look and smell nice.

Disciples   Followers of a great person.

Florists   People who work in flower shops.

Goddesses   Female gods.

Holy   Specially for worship.

Juno   A Roman goddess, the wife of Jupiter.

Linen   Goods such as towels, sheets and tablecloths.

Second World War   The war that lasted from 1939–45.

Spices   Flavours for food.

Victorian   During the reign of Queen Victoria (1837–1901).

Further information

A Sense of History, Every Year by
Sallie Purkis (Longman, 1995)

Festivals of the Christian Year by
Lois Rock (Lion Books, 1996)

Get Set Go! Spring Festivals by
Helen Bliss (Watts, 1995)

Index

Americans 20, 21, 22

cards 5, 22, 23, 24, 25, 28
chocolates 5

Easter 9, 19

flowers 5, 6, 8, 16, 26, 27

gifts 6, 16, 22

helping out 5, 29

Jarvis, Miss Anna 20
Jesus Christ 10, 18, 19
Juno 7

Lent 9, 10, 11

Mother Church 8, 11
Mother Nature 6
Mothering Sunday meal 12–13

Romans 7

Simnel cake 17, 18, 19